R. J. Dillon

R. J. Dillon has written in one form or another for most of his professional life, firstly as a copywriter, then as an academic and latterly as a full-time writer of fiction. Born in the North West of England, he obtained a first class honours degree in English and History from Manchester Polytechnic, an MA in Visual Culture from Lancaster University where he also successfully completed a Ph.D in History. He is married with two children and lives on the Lancashire coast, where he devotes his time to writing, walking and reading.

rjdillon.com

twitter.com/RJ_Dillon

About this collection

Midnight's Revolution marks the fruition of a personal journey spanning over twenty-three years. What began as fragmented, intimate recollections, gradually became a series of voices to deal with a conflicting array of emotions, experiences and disappointments.

I make no claim to be a poet, simply a writer who has, for better or worse, attempted to use aspects of the poetic form as a means of expression, a humble offering of an open dialogue to be shared.

The poems are not organised into any chronological order, merely allocated a place in each of the sections that seemed most appropriate. Some originate from my creative writing course – expertly taught by the British poet Jeffrey Wainwright – as part of my undergraduate degree. Others reflect different periods and events; the miscarriage of our first child, the death of my parents, the absurdity of life.

Unlike my novels and non-fiction work, this form of writing offers little room to hide behind characters or historical facts and interpretation. Raw, genuine and sometimes too honest, the collection is my voice amongst many and I take full responsibility for their inflection, their utterances. I therefore apologise in advance if I have failed to communicate or ultimately disappoint.

By the same author

The Oktober Projekt

The Fanatic

Hunted and Damned

Non-fiction

History on British television: Constructing nation, nationality and collective memory

Midnight's Revolution

R. J. Dillon

R
Revidion

Published by
Revidion 2012

British Library Cataloguing in Publication Data. A
catalogue record for this book is available from the British
Library.

ISBN: 978 0 9572651 3 4

For Jeffrey Wainwright

Thank you for nourishing the spark

Contents

TERRITORY OF THE SOUL

THE HOUSE OF LIFE

SHAPES IN THE NIGHT

TERRITORY OF THE SOUL

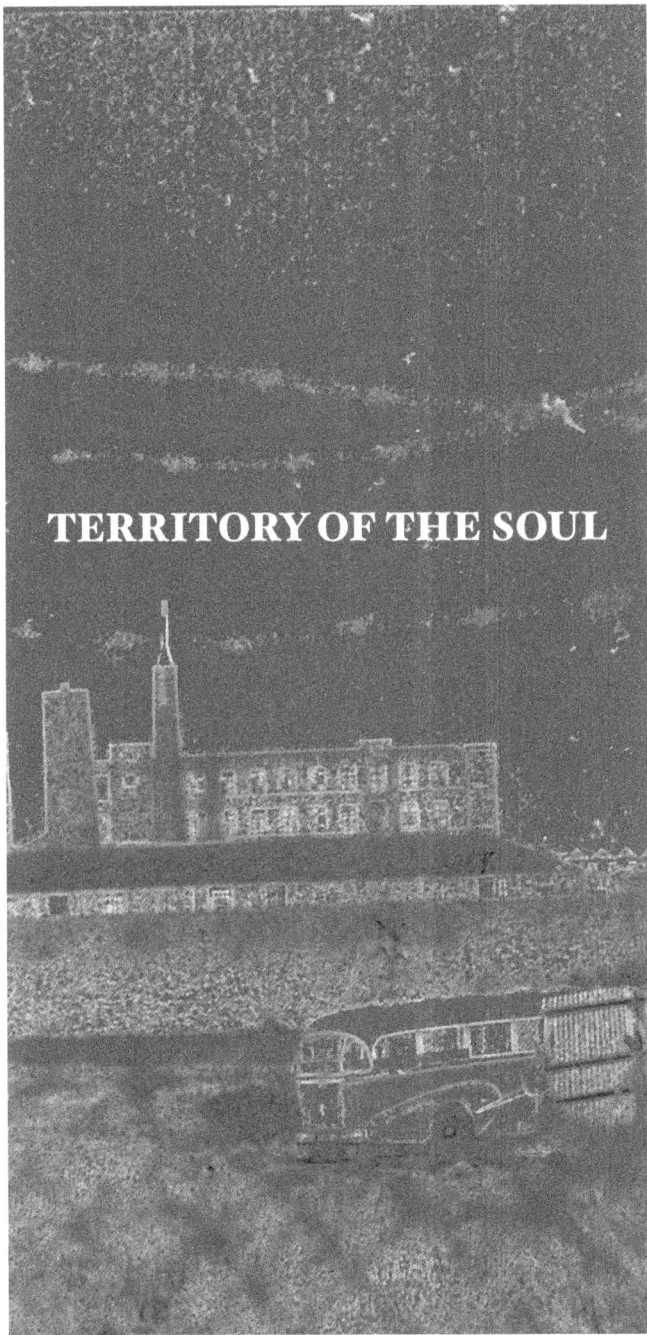

SAND

And sheltering, we rested, flicked
flat into shadows, warm hands
slapping
the mossy ODEON wall. Sand
trapped under
our fingernails,
your hair wet, dribbling against
my cheek.

We lose touch, sense our drift.

Our breath flows in bloated ribbons,
curling remotely
into pewter clouds so heavy,
breathing becomes a sin.
Soon we will go.

Divided,
unrepentant from our own
requirements to occupy other lives,
we masquerade
as squatters on stars yet to be
discovered.

LOST CHILD

I let you down, not urgently responding
to each desperate kick, only passing
on my fluid breath, somehow corrupt,
suspending you in ambivalence, subtly growing,

until you fell under their spell. *Chthonic*
interlopers seeking out tokens, stealing
souls to feed an undisclosed master.
Lost in this world underground, you had

no answer. I could only numbly watch
as Kronos taught by favour, feasted on infants
deposited in the square. Children old before
their allotted time, movement suspended.

Simple touches of finger to finger they once
transmitted inside their sealed drum
withered, turned slack. The last rites of
Proserpine, played to a full house.

Respectable but clean, honest but
too early for their own good,
four men true and solid enter the square,
their burnished scalpels daubing the sun.

Women cloaked from death, see life pass
down their legs and weep pity they've never
claimed. The gaps between belly
and true mind encompass all they own.

Ears split by screams from hearts of
fire, listening to nothing save

Rune fables cast out into the wilderness.
Barren thoughts becalmed in a sea of dreams,

floating but never still. Free falling
into paradise where a sacred mother bore
an early child, its lips burst, smothering
entrails with rotten fingers as it sang of life.

Take me to paradise where kingfishers
feast on relics of the mind. Tattered
thoughts never to speak phonetically of
a scream plundering the flesh bearing tomb.
Nothing left – save one child.

God forbid – forbid God. Free knowledge
from withered hands crabbing at the soil.
Earth of the moon blighted by Zeus on a
star damned by stillborn cries.

No more. Drift aimless across tracks
of waste. Nuclear pay dirt of the future
 – mined by hands scrubbed clean and
spared pain. Thrusting pain, conception –

mutation in a coffin, darkness and silent
dreams that deliver an unformed limb,
from bloody door to bloody door.
Agony, sufferance of the still unborn.

Negotiations to 'sturb the dead. Eliot?
Is that you again? Come at last to make
your deal? Talk over the future in a square mile
of waste. Take my child it is already dead.

YESTERDAY'S HEROES

Fumes from a paraffin lamp
glisten in my head.
To look forward is ripened
seed sucked dry by the
humming bee of efficiency.
Sending letters of brown
recycled paper, invariably
torn, they try to make amends.

'The law states,' how much I
 am entitled to suffer.

Fact is son, you ain't got
the class to lick their
spoon.

But how do they know of my
tokens stored – knowledge, loss,
butchery for my monarch, my
social role as pariah?

Tick-box lunar men and women,
with cosmic eyes duller
than black dwarf stars.
What is the tariff
for surviving one night on
this stinking planet?
What is the price for
never asking to be born?

THE VISION

I feel strong at the lake's edge,
deep water takes my breath's weight.
Slowly, cartwheeling into sound I
sense the urgency, feel your laugh
torn from my grasp, then emerge, a
hundred tongueless voices tossed
inside my head.

The wonder. Why did I let him go?
Only to surface, cold, frozen
out of memory, out of purpose,
useless on a block.

It was Fra Lippi's last night,
tortured, torn and returned to
rationality by your reciting of
his fears.

Failure is to die without
knowing your father. Yes, you said that.
And more.

I touch mud unstirred by hands,
layered pigments too frail for decades
of uncritical stares. A clouded canvas;
Virgin Mary Blue, yes, the true blood
of Christ. If only it were true. Brown, I
see no more. Ochre then,
a shade to deceive, but please,
remember the lies when I arise
and proclaim a vision.

I DON'T NEED IT

I don't need
the clattering rattle of his Pontius
tongue in his empty head, his smile,
a knife
deftly thrust between my ribs,
his arrogance, momentarily dissolved,
waiting for a second chance.

I don't need
his blunt barbs scraping through
my brain, picking for inspiration, trying
to resolve an inadequacy, to
complement
the illusion of being the 'best', to save a
decadent ego suckered on self-righteous
pap.

I don't need
his eclectic knowledge chimed
every hour, his lust for subjects, his
comfort,
his desire for power, his time: an
eternity,
every second clubbed into submission
by a hammer blow of boredom until the
day
screams for release.

I don't need
confrontation on what I can do,
dictated by his aversion to the truth.
His trust
in all things written in time past has
burnt my eyes with his puckered
resolution never to charm; but to
become a blur, the flashing of
someone who thinks he's
written bigger than GOD!

I don't need
his modern usage for 'love' to settle
disputes, to launch another
encyclopaedic
rip-off, for the pain causes yet another
constellation to collapse somewhere in
my heart.

I don't need his life – full stop.

NOTHING MORE TO BE SAID

Expressionless,
unless I relate a death.
Of how I drove unseeing,
unknowing into the past,
tears filling gaps,
dropping unmanly on my
lap.

Oh, you will never know
again the touch of green,
a cloud pattern or a breeze's
smothering lick... or the
pain.
Real enough, you were quite
right.
My pain, the guilt,
intolerable, of having
arrived too late.

Nowhere to park and you
going
fast. More tears, looks of
pity turning
to strange intent. But I had
to run.
Corridors the same but not
the one I want.
Young doctors wait, a small
room, a beating clock
and flowers abandoned after

the fact.
White coated efficiency.
They explain
the worst, still medical
school dumb to deal
with death.

Real death, your death.

The ward buzzed over its
lunch: sausage, fish, or cold
ham.
And cold you were,
unknown behind a soft wall
of patterned fabric.

Unseen, ignored by life's rich
routine,
but the faintest smile
surviving
for your only son.

NORTHERN LIGHTS

Silent sheds of
Northern lights,
backs to the sun.

Sledge hammers
arc through lazy
noon-lulled dust.

Fly wheels fall
onto shuttle tips
leaking polished rust.

Flagstones bleached
by tackler's piss
wait by the truck.

Pulley belts hang in
cracked shafts of
ruptured time.

Lipped talk – 'Did he?'
'You never!' clings to
stone walls cushioned by
spittle cotton coughed
from ailing lungs.

Pipes, bred, lagged
and cosseted for steam
are cold to touch,
the hissing stopped.

Boilers, belly-fed,
rot, suck at a distant sky
through brick straws
pressed into slubbed cloud.

Mute memories replace the beat
of mechanical hearts;
iron pulses that once
tapped out a golden future.

THINK IT, DON'T SAY IT

Some things you just
Don't mention. Debt, health,
Salary; why haven't you conjured-up children?

Colour of hair, skin, body form,
Shape, age depreciation. When was
Your first kiss, real sexual encounter?

Mental agility, intellectual deficiency?
Speaking your mind risks committing a hate
Crime.

Laws govern our tongues, shape our thoughts,
Speech is no longer a freedom, but
A prison.

THE LIVING

I died today and no one noticed.
A broken smile cut into dry lips,
deformed, unprepared for
midnight's song, its revolution.

To sleep, I want for nothing more.
But what peace can you trace
on walls of faded roses when damp
slithers by. Underfed, trickling dirty
tears of little purpose, of no regret...
and yet...
remember yet...

Beetles skid across the floor,
coal skinned, hardy to rot
they trail decay into corners never
touched, never seen by throwers of
posies, the knot of friends who dash
remembrance ash onto
the box.

Tell me then, of velvet leaves
brittle to touch, of soft rain,
of stems slender, of earth corrupt. So it
crumbled in my fingers, smattered my
shoes, drifted out of touch.
Forgetting where and when
is only the beginning.

I scan faces sometimes, and they
smile. Their breath etched on my
marble, streams away in cracked

tongues, trembling from the effort.
Twice a day from work and home,
the stones rattling at their passing.
If they care to look they will see a
shadow sitting on air.

But my spirit smirks behind their
backs and so I press scoured eyelids
into lips. Sleep, peace, sleep now.
But there is no night, only blue light
skimmed from a cold sea burning
my eyes with its beating waves.

Turning, darkness shoulders a bare
arm about my silhouette, pats dry
my earth walls and drops a stain into
the hole. Sleep is a dream so long
ago.

FLUKE OF BIRTH

Him?
King-fluke of a rain misted land,
fertile in mind, barren in hand.
His dormant seed sniggers at my youth
brittle with age. I have no time, no
temper for his learned wise men,
grovelling, cracked, dishevelled at my
brother's feet. Muzzled bitches snarl at
empty hours; lost scents, warm flesh,
drooling for the master's cackle. Preying
birds unleashed for fun, tug and tear
at ruptured eyes; tattered corneas flap
beside balustraded slabs supporting his
sterile throne. A yawn and they are gone,
one wasted nation, my life a distant
meridian.

'*Woruldstrenga binom waette sippan*', chimes
his tame funny man; the world is water,
help me I'm drowning.

Outstretched on a divan, his wasted
shadow dances, fumed by candles, his
body my mausoleum. Attracted by King-
whispered favours, women basqued,
stockinged, stilettoed, compete to win
one grin from his frozen withered lips.
A scholastic chemist, producer of gold,
admits defeat over my brother's poxed
corrupted core. Lifeless, ice-filled, his
corpse pulses mottled blood through

leper limbs unstirred by passion. Dear brother you take this final journey on your own, a golden raft to ride Lethe's currents. What I did, I did in the name of this corrupted nation.

UNSAID

The unsaid hangs
between us,
a gossamer of dread.
My life reiterated,
Past, Present,
No Future.

Unsaid in the past,
explanations,
key-note phrases
that would allow me
to express my unhappiness,
my painful ignorance.
That you lied, cheated
away our pleasure on a sultry whim,
spent time with HIM, converting love
into stolen copulating hours.

Presently unsaid, but rattling
in my head. Thank you for
cutting my life into threads,
for the figure of eight slashed
through every bone,
severing vessels ferrying blood.

Watching myself from the future,
I am a ghost of all that happened.
In a blazer and cavalry twill
trousers hitched high,

I wear carpet slippers holed at both toes.
My gentle rhythmic breathing summons
the undead wearing tarnished haloes.
Smiling, I wedge my door into its hole,
I scuffle forwards.
'You loved me once.' My voice tuneless,
every note punctured.

Two silver buttons hang from my blazer,
on the sleeve a long crusty scab of dried
snot. I rake my sparse hair with a mottled,
liver spotted hand, waiting for your answer.

But all you provide is a laugh, step up,
embrace my shadow, stab me once more
in the back, this time smiling.

BE MY FRIEND

'I know you're there, I
have this feeling of you
behind me all the time...
Can feel your shadow sharp,
nestled into my back, the tension
of your hands sifting my hair...
of being followed by my best friend...
hear your footsteps rise on each
stair....'

        'It's all in your mind.'

'It's true, weird really.
Sometimes when I stare
through my mirror...
I've the same sensation...
of you there... at my side...
Breathing in pain, your eyes
hazy, like you saw me for
the first time...'

        'That's creepy.'

'Sometimes in bed at night...
I see your shape stretched before me...
it's like... it's like your carrying
an axe.'

        'Now you're having a laugh.'

But it's true, and on my pillow I see a face.
Yours, printed; a pale blood smeared
impression on soft calico, your lips in a
sneer, a last protest at my smile.

THE HOUSE OF LIFE

AUGUST STORM

The waves rouse me,
a womb pulse swaying
gently forward, back,
covering molten rock
hard set by a million
tides of equinox passing.
(Granite longing for
spume to lick its wounds).

Each wave dulls the
ache inside my head
smoothing tissue raw
with heat. Lamps burning
still time, drop smoky
shadows to greet
darkness nudging adobe
sand thin walls.

A child's breath slides
by me, into the valley where
a woman once loved sings
to the sun. A broken story
drowned by drumming thunder,
distant, a lifetime off. I stare
along wind tucked ridges
at blue forks charging home
alone.

A lizard pads cornerwise to
shelter, thousands of storms
trapped in one prehistoric
form. My palms itch, stain
the leather arms of the
window seat still creased
from where she used to sit
frowning at August storms.

Trumpet vines shudder,
stems erect, as shots
of thunder part sullen air.
In a second of erupted
light I view our valley
stripped clean, scarred
rock on sand, a path of
mulberry leaves where we met.

Then against rocks in a
dashing echo, the Atlantic
mutters. Someday water will
succeed, kiss the shore no
more so we will all have
peace. Enter then my
memory teased by heat

into a charred script of
ashen-youth. Of promises
broken, and week-long nights
recalling blushes formed on
a wink. I still see her
bare shoulders, and tidy hair
before we toured despair
together and alone.

Waiting for rain, dregs
of age pile unripe seeds in
a jar where Mothers die -
old trees toppling into a
marsh with the drip,
drip, drip of leaking
time. Each drop a
lie from father to son.

At last, fist-sized storm
splashes plant wishes in
dungy beetle ruts. A futile
task, but I hold back, touch
spines exposed, pages bare,
volumes of printed dust
on a shelf held by weary
nails. Thunder shakes us all.

The chill is sudden
to my skin after weeks
of locust torn air.
Sounds of return follow
water through furrows
cracking seed. Somewhere in
approaching dawn, a dog barks
at the disappearing storm.

DEAR MOTHER, SORRY BUT...

'...you've gone at last.'
After all this time, the
distance
travelled, only to discover at
the end, life isn't a
blast, it's nothing more than
futile resistance.

'Isn't she pretty, her fine
dress,
remember it? Her summer
frock she called it.'
Her being here was not to
acquiesce or
reject what little difference
any of us make.

'The Beads? my idea, bought
on our honeymoon.'
Imagine, all those years... of
not knowing
what separates us from
darkness until we have
nothing to see but glow stick
shadows casting out our
ragged obligations.

There we sit until called,
revenants stacked on
numbered shelves.
'Touch her if you like,
Don't mind her being cold.'

KINETICS
OF LOVE

One touch ignites a resonance.
Forged only once, our invisible bond
stamps an act of union between time,
place, even questions of reckoning.

Where will we be in ten years time?

Is it an inseparable fusion, a molten base
for the Kinetics of Love? Or
just infatuation, juvenile
misrepresentation?
Flowing between flesh and dreams it

weaves circles through time, insisting on
one of us knowing who is real, who the
simulacrum.
We sat together in that unruly state,
caught in the fizz of loves' dog bite
hallucination.

Did we ever answer that question?

Behind us a life to be lived
by others who
don't know us, never will.
In front of us, crossing
the ledge of moor, summer's weary eye
already
had our measure,

calculating, smugly offering
light or shade, a choice,
a shared fate. Clouds
yoked to a screaming wind,
a whole continent
on the move disguising
the birdsong of
wanton destruction.

What would have
become of us if we'd stayed together?

One of us would inflict the wound,
a turn of the head, slyly glance the other
way,
shuddering at a touch, a softly broken
word.
Then with dry lips it would end with a
Judas kiss.

OPEN PRISON

The streets function as our prison,
guarded by a remote all-seeing wisdom,
sentinels for every season fixed, fast, forever
mechanically offering a reflective glare.
A cold-hearted opinion on the difference
between right and wrong, craning out
to crimes where victims are a blur.

Twenty-four hour vision, robotic
resolution, panning, zooming for
no other reason but they're there.
Controlled by operators passing sentence
without remorse or defence,
trial by closed-circuit television.

HUMAN ZOO

Every city exhibits
its own unique collection,
it's just a matter of knowing
where to find them.
If you're free on Saturday
night, I'd recommend the
command performance.
Take your ticket, fill out the form,
wait in line for
endless hours of entertainment.
Don't bother with the matinée,
connoisseurs never miss midnight's
show at our local
Accident and Emergency.

Tonight's acts are varied,
requiring minimal introduction.

In a corner a middle-aged pair
huddle on plastic chairs,
the woman silently weeping,
the man drawn, pale, convulsing.
Cornered by two nurses
a girl in her teens with blood -
spattered bandages clamped
around her wrists spits and curses.
'Come on love, calm down.'

Snarling and laughing,
the girl's electric eyes
burn off the booze,
drugs or glue firing her

internal spark, defining
her very being, fuelling her
rebellious system.

Stumbling in out of a taxi,
a women in her fifties enters
centre stage, automatic doors parting
as if taking her final curtain.
Greeting everyone with a wave,
she rejects offers of help, strutting
amongst ranks of awed spectators.

Under her raincoat she parades
nothing but tattered strips
of a dirty waist slip,
sloughed down around
the eight-inch heels bought to
please her new bloke.
'Your a thief and liar,' she endlessly bawls
into a cracked make-up mirror,
lightly cradled to her breast,
a surrogate replacement
for children long since
swallowed by the State.

Around this tawdry chaos,
a team of cleaners fan out
through banks of packed seats.
Synchronised sweeping,
the efficient brushing away
of human detritus.
Murmuring in dark
corners, violent shadows
dance out of tune, partial remains
of once whole individuals who
wilfully refuse to conform.

DELIVERANCE

He wretched once, before me
on his hands and knees, an all-too familiar
Benediction.

Blackened knuckles white to the bone
supported his weight, amounting
to nothing.

Swivelling, using stumps of fingers
spread as uselessly as paws, one hollowed eye
blinked in recognition.

He wretched again, this time in
words. Love's lost pledges,
tripped out from a moth-savaged

tapestry, the binding around his guilt-edged vault
of adult secrets. His relics of devotion,
talismans of reconciliation.

Around him, possessions I had never known:
sleeping bag rolled, bound in cord, begging card
written in an addictive hand.

Mixed in the copper valley of his blanket, gobbets
of spit from passers-by scared to admit how love
lost between mother and son isn't an illusion.

I REMEMBER WHEN...

We held hands without
thinking about duty,
a sense of commitment.
Kissed on the lips, fully, not
pretending. Laughed when
we opened our wedding
presents, planned for a life
spared of second guessing.
We shared our dreams
together free from deceit,
not manoeuvring behind
coyote shrieks and mute-
eyed excuses.

We held conversations, never
levelled accusations, guarded
our time together as a valued
possession. Blamed others
for any misfortune, regarded
time as an accomplice, not a
wilful obstruction.
We never had silences
deeper than screams,
embarrassment
from a brush of shoulders,
your skin dusting mine.

When we lay together,
comfortable, unguarded,
our sleeping breaths mutual
reassurance, our bodies
shaped into one resolute
being. Hendrix guarded our
primal desire from along his
electric Watchtower, unaware
of impending fragmentation.
We looked forward,
never back, we whispered
compliments, not acid-
tipped laments, we never
believed in solo retreats or
recriminations.

I remember when we were
one being.

LIFE'S PRISM

What little we know of life
from inside vanity's soft prism.
When we're cheating time from
11-19 every day is a flavoured heaven.

Tomorrow is always prepared,
a hessian blur, a photograph
waiting to be stored, uploaded,
shared around as ammunition.
Friends are recycled, meaningless
ghosts prodded, poked,
tagged in thousands.

Ambulances are what
old people catch,
death is a sequence
that you watch
on the laptop, tablet, phone
or at the multiplex.
Reality isn't real, it's a
franchise on TV.

Appearance is all-important,
never left to luck
or nature. ME is a pronoun,
symbolic interjection
and personal
statement, admired in loving
reflected glances from

passing cars, windows,
imagining premieres and
celebrity weddings.

Old age has lost its gravity.
Its moons, its suns,
its visions of infirmity
dismissed with a cyber click.

But it's there, patiently
waiting with its brittle poke,
life's enduring joke packed
with blemishes,
the certain promise
of reducing generations
of idealised, pampered
seed to dust.

IDEAL HOME

Dressed in deep red, visibility
For the dispossessed, each morning
Takes them on a visit to a cell block.

Inmates roused, peer incoherently
Between open bars of daylight.
Clutching their bags warmed by
Sleep, they nod answers, mumble assurances
About their wellbeing.

Cell after cell visited, checking,
Toting up the human damage, advice
Offered, rarely taken.

Being homeless comes at a price,
On each cell: OCCUPIED scrolled in bold,
Twenty pence transforming public
Lavatories into personal hotels.
The red-cloaked guardians
Have their list of inmates,
Regulars who one morning
May fail to respond, refuse life's
Roll call.

TOWER
BLOCKS

After a couple of centuries
gap, I stand transfixed,
mesmerized by their
aspect. Looking up at their
long standing will to defeat
the object of survival,
the intimate collusions
between earth and heaven,
the destructive forces
of generations pushed
into their concrete hips,
their swaggering tips,
the rods of purpose
holding up their heads
of fine tempered steel,
of mortared base bricks
licked by the spit of the
red-neck youths who come
to walk in circles of light,
obscured by their blind
belief in ending what their
mother started.

Inside there is Faith, an
ideal woman,
the mother of a generation
locked in incubation.
Hearing their wails, she
spins apocalyptic visions
on turntables, reads the

glossy pages, discusses
the beneficial merits of a
spliff or two, measures the
diameter of her universe
with a myopic view from
her end of the world
balcony through a fisheye
lens delivering news that
raising one-night open
legged children turns a
curse into a blessing. Up
there, remote, unfettered
by humanity, the chains of
social order, she counts her
lucky stars, relishing this
crazy world where no man
is coming between a Holy
Mother and her streetwise
children.

WALK

Walk Goddamn you...

I walk in anger, not regret, a slow march,
toting my soul in a paper sack.
Through my cracked eyes,
I visualise life flash frying time.

Black sky, no sun, only rain. Seasons
of a pierced mind, the dead territory
of my heart. Cars pass in endless strands,
a rosary bead of colour – sunburst viridian,

satin, crimson. There are no lights
this side of heaven, everything defined
through an internal fog.
But I don't mind, I am not alone

in this land of honeycombed blight.
A dog pads through the square, walked by
a woman in pyjamas, her dressing
gown open. It's cold, the streets an auditorium

of frost. Spun strips of snow sting
my fingers, plants icy tubers inside my brain,
transforming each step into a slurred
parody of a shuffle. My body belongs to another,

a tenant not prepared for the journey,
my legs mutant blocks of skin, no bone.
I lay down without a shout,
this is time running out.

LOST YOUTH'S ANTHEM

They descend every Saturday night,
claiming streets, entire pavements.
Snorting exuberance, their eyes alight
in the ritual of chasing oblivion.

Every move fluid, choreographed,
a dynamic performance. Bodies primed
on liquid bravado, mesh and bind,
primitive instincts unsheathed.

An army stripped of inhibition
advancing, shod and clad in off-the-peg
fatigues,
they circle, traversing through furtive
primal manoeuvres, pure endurance.

Shouts, yells, screams; their tribal
whoops
stake territorial ownership. One more
nocturnal right of passage rooted in
open seismic defiance.

Juiced-up, livers and brains bursting,
egos suffering heightened stimulation,
only self-preservation courses through
bloated veins in doomed regimentation.

There are no generals, only foot soldiers,
warrior drunks snarling rebukes,

their curses pure venom, thrown fast
with the ferocity of a punch.

Flashing tits, bums, cocks and balls
is never discouraged, it's cherished,
a battle honour. Blood, vomit, piss
and body fluid – another box ticked.

This their final fling before falling
into a taxi, licking kebab tinted
fingers; knowing this is their Great
Britain, this their heritage, our loss of
freedom.

SHAPES IN THE NIGHT

RELICS OF THE MOOR

Close your eyes and see them,
not as shadows on sepia tints
encapsulated in nostalgia,
but callused skin, pitted bone,
faces filthy rag mops from living.
Bodies grafted from gritstone,
sculpted by privation, of boundaries known,
exceeded through desperation.

This broken pile belonged to them,
overgrown ribs of hand-cut base stone
their home. Sliced into moorland, nothing neat
but life planted on a savage hillside
where little remains. Not skin, not bone,
just footprints of walls, a hint
of an opening where weary stooped
shadows entered. Soles of grass hummocks
where they broke each day's monotony
in their dry-stone citadel staring from
arrow slit windows.

Huddled in a bunch, woman, man, children,
bleeding courage when storms beat their door,
threatening to wash them off the moor.
Crafted into a corner, their High Altar,
its reredos soot seared from stunted flame
nourished by blunt fingers stubborn with pain.
Of their daily Eucharist rabbit, grouse or pheasant,
nothing remains, their ciborium now open sky,
scattered bones the only after-feast relics.

WAVES

Powerful, an endless corrosive tide
Sobbing at the shores of humanity.
Twice a day they mount their attack
An army dragging its feet across pebble,
Shingle, sand, battering their foaming
Heads against bluffs, open beach and cliffs.

Standing there, remote, knowing that
There is nothing to be done in defence
Clears the head of adulation. This is reality,
Uncompromising recognition that as feeble
Beings we do not actually make a difference.

The longer I remain, hearing the hiss, surge
Of breakers, my fingers numb, cheeks coated
In spume, each crashing pulse corrects my own
Minute ambition. The wind becomes a second-
Skin, serenading me with whispers of voyages
I never will take.

NOT NYMPHS

Sometimes you glimpse them
locked in one corner of your eye.
Haggard bean faces, split, siphoned into
fissures, oblivious in their ignorance of life
spent in submission.

None of them blessed with Calpurnia's
vision. Each a solo sufferer, walled open
mouthed into tabernacles of pain.
Their life-shells drained by existence,
these are not children of any revolution,
just walking corpses offering no resistance.

Blink twice and they readily transform,
inward torment publicly disgorged.
Flickering manifestations of chained
nymphs, tallow-faced Caménae morphed
into *The Scream*.

The external agony of being true
to themselves, unlocks their minds'
inarticulate composition.

Listen to their broken nails slash
a cross on a blackboard, scoring out a
bland philosophy, a compass needle
hovering between death, deceit, survival.

Once blinked alive, they become
impossible to shift. Their stitched eyes

see nothing of knowing, sitting squat in
corners addled by shadows, blind tears fall
into the palms of grasping hands
as if snatching a ball.

Sequined lips sparkle with empty promise,
siren calls filter through hollow squares
of the night, ready to scarify any
life a little less ordered.
These are not Nymphs.

THE GREEN BENCH

After school there is
thought Only of You.
Panic, a hole in my
universe, my life dark
after someone had stolen
the sun.

So my solitary trek is
undertaken halfway
between man and boy for
my journey to The Green
Bench. I wait, stomach cramped,
muscles in free-fall, turmoil in
mind, body, soul. I wait,
a stunted guard
of honour, a sentry of one,
nursing my longing in the evening
trimmed in winter's dark fur.

My senses in a knot, a diurnal
fatigue as I wait for the headlights,
a hunger that you will never leave me
raids my store of belief, my will
to understand. But the waiting adds to
my craving, I taste only the cold, fumes of
passing traffic as the night suffocates
my refuge, threatens my lifeboat built
for me alone, my Green Bench inside
the bus shelter.

Not yet ten but I understand
something about loss. The bodies queuing,
those speeding by with someone waiting
to meet them, make each one
whole again.

I know the regulars in my shelter;
the man stunted by half a face who is
embarrassed,
ashamed on my behalf,
the girls laughing
at how they will become women.
None of us know
each other, but none
of us are strangers,
The Green Bench inside
the bus shelter is our home,
our sanctuary, our shared
delusion.

A DATE WITH DESTINY

Riddled with expectation, he waits
everyday for this moment of salvation.
Love from a distance, Destiny unknowing,
an object of devotion, his fantasy, his escape.

An outline, a sky-formed silhouette,
she is nothing more. To him she is
Everything. Her figure entirely drafted from
his imagination, Destiny is his creation.

Wife, mother, daughter, lover,
He has amalgamated her from shards
of personal history. Her eyes, hair
the shape of her chin, cheeks, jaw

all converge into a smile that once
welcomed him home. He isn't a voyeur,
merely a devoted admirer, an ardent
flâneur mistakenly believing he exists.

When she appears on the distant
hill, tending her horses, he raises
one arm covertly in salute, hoping
she knows nothing of his admiration.

Now her stables serve as a shrine
for his romantic relief, the untaxed love that
brings no VAT, no surcharge. Can dreams
carry that far, cover so much distance?

They have never met but he knows
there is a bond.

Invisibly transmitted in the air,
crackling with premature devotion,
it requires nerves he doesn't
possess to bridge the gap.

An injection of love to travel so far, span
each dusty decade? Discovered at the
window, hands grip his chair. The spell
broken, tears rise, but in his defiance he
refuses to please them.

'You trying to escape again, dear?' one of
them chimes.
'Let's put you back where you belong,'
laughs her shallow friend, wheeling him
full circle into the residents' lounge for
more of his life-tomb of care,
returned for his date with Destiny.

OUR LIVES

When our lives
Contained nothing but summer,
You promised to remember me.
Now your skeletal hands of memory
Have grown tired of their pledge,
Gorged themselves on others.

You talk now out of love, not in
Romantic riddles, but cold Morse
And semaphore; a crackling code
For you alone, with me
Left mute, receiving but
Never transmitting.

Where do I stand in your thoughts,
As an echo of communication?
How do I rate as a memory when the
Filters of the past are irredeemably
Locked,
The blood of our once
Cherished code broken, frozen.

STONE

They are a race hewn out of stone,
spewed from the rocky hump
of England's middle loin. Scars of crag, fell,
shale, bastard hard gritstone – these are
children of molten fusion, the ancient stock
caressed to mould the Pennines.

Boulders, rocks, flat-faced slabs beaten
open every season, reared without fingers
ringed from mercurial success.
A solid backbone burnt, frozen, wind
scoured and washed, pushing up, out
of its shimmering skin of grass.

Abandoned below worm kissed earth,
moss and hazy distant heather, their
stagnant womb-sack caves. They do
not care for sentiment, these children
of glacial birth. Their carboniferous
parents have pledged them air, water, earth.

Nutrients enough to grow uncontaminated,
unconcerned. Permanent sentinels with dark
scoured faces grizzled shut in winter storms,
year after year they migrate. Knuckles buried
into dank moss they gyrate north, south,
east or west, one slithering inch at a time.

The precocious ones, wild brats without fear,

are propped nonchalantly on their haunches,
walls of ancient molten action trapped,
frozen between sheets of sod and cloud.
Calling, always calling into skeetering winds,
whispering rebukes, questioning their birth,
asserting their right to guard their Earth.

IN CELEBRATION

An engagement party or something of the
sort... the host, Glen – promoted the night
before – I don't frankly remember, greets
everyone with a snort;
leads the way with his beer gut
parting guests: 'Coming thru', a determined
juggernaut of pampered flesh.

Small, he makes up his lack of height
as a professional cynic, a walking wrecking
ball who nods, smiles; his cold pigeon eyes a
blight, assaying everyone, calculating value,
opposition.

Mandy is Glen's childhood girlfriend, his
beloved Princess locked in her corner dipped
in matt screen shadow, monitoring her
betrothed, her piercing hawk eyes
sharper than a jilted lover's. Like Glen, she
is small, a willow, her hair combed perfectly
into long winceyette strands, her lips never
over-strained, nursing her drink, forming a
grudge against marriage.

Uncle Oswald is down from Edinburgh or
Glasgow, I don't frankly remember... much...
except that he's train mad
and I'm pinned against a sideboard.
He rattles them off; numbers, sets

of wheels, famous runs, names
of locomotives,
even Dear God,
infamous level crossings.

Smiling at my
mute enthusiasm he nods
across the room. 'That's my
adopted boy.'
I follow his proud claim,
rotating,
turning,
until I see through
a needle gap in remote tangled bodies,
a child perhaps ten.
Blind, with no legs, rocking constantly on a
chair where he recognises every voice, each
face. His looks, his Divine interpretation
transcends. He understands, recognises
the signs, hears everything not as a
celebration, but as a prelude
to a Requiem.

HEARD AND NOT SEEN...

...are sounds from my window. Each night's
vacant stillness acting as an amplifier,
broadcasting life beyond my reason.

Motorbikes... cars... mostly, speed into the
night's renegade core. Leaving no clues
behind, they eat their way into the distance
riding on a wall of sound.

Journeys taut with individual beginnings
and no logical end, my world and theirs
constructed in different tongues, travellers
from opposing universes.

I imagine their faces, reasons for traversing
across the night's sticky embrace. I
reconstruct their lives; family, friends, who
they are meeting, why
they must go.

MEMORY

Inside the mind's bone-can,
memories are spliced,
reworked into kaleidoscope
segments of life
wilfully resisting natural order.

Edited of smell,
touch; devoid of pain,
they stagnate into decaying
scars of remembrances taunting
our ideal reflection.

Delicate soft tissue ruptured
releases moments of life.
Slithering forward, an uncoiled worm
of inconsistency, they mutate. Forgotten
parts consume each other until nothing
remains,

but a bloated stain. A highway of polluted
discovery bearing not one framed shot
of reality. Montages barely seen,
unscripted scenes, interlopers
playing all the main parts.

These translucent dreams are famished,
fossilised within this bone-can
of my mind. The flimsy fabric
of memory stirs, starts to rise,
then deflates, the projector runs on idle.

Becalmed into a sea of false dreams
every wave
washes me with torment
of what passed, what
could have been.

THE NEXT TRAIN

Creeping towards Accrington
my train ages to a crawl, breathing in the
curve, delivering me into a past from where
I departed at a quite different station.
Pressed up against smeared exit glass,
waiting for the lurch, the platform stop,
I receive my first shock, sharper than hands
choking midnight on my mind's clock.

Uttered silently, a wounded disclaimer:
No... this isn't what I remember, how it began.
Shape-shifting planners have purged my
inner core, feasted on blood, bone,
tissue, on what made me what I am.

Not quite a traveller from a distant land,
but I quickly confirm this as my own
Ozymandias. A landscape so familiar
I knew it by smell now festers, a work in
progress, an unfinished canvas,
colours smeared by craven hands.

Trickles of brutal sweat linger in pools,
obliterated streets, grammar schools,
churches of redemption, smudged into
oblivion. This poached carcass leaking
industrial dust, writhes in revolt beside the
track, its butchered remains picked clean

after development hunters divvied up their
spoils. And from the weeds
bloom modern flowers, none bursting poppy
red seeds to grow another generation of Pals,
this harvest sprouts wavy tin cladded roofs
fitted over concrete shells.

Red bricks of fire, stone masked, baked in
soot, this is how I'd preserved my landscape,
my heritage, images gestated into a resolution
to return. I drag my feet, find an excuse, a
missed call, change counted,
anything to absent myself from re-entering
this strange sea not inked on my faded
charts. Back in the skeletal embrace
of my childhood mausoleum, I tread currents
avoiding mortal inhibition, realise this is a
mistake. Hiding excuses in pockets
stuffed with exotic visas, I mouth my tired
silent chorus: *Did I escape because I'm a coward?*

Grudgingly I mount angle-iron steps, stop,
fully at the footbridge's centre, stripped back
to shivering bare iron bands, its roof rimed
in holiday laughter dismantled, glass steam-
cleaned, rinsed in smoke, removed for health
and safety, I suppose.

I risk one last panoramic reintroduction.
This is grief, genuine nostalgia, echoes
trapped inside a split personality.
The flash photography of childhood
burrowed deep, wormed away for morbid
pleasure, rapidly fading under
the stark glare of a Lancashire mill town I

thought I once knew.
The lodge where summer was fished,
girls kissed, dens built in lush, strange
undergrowth of head-high grass,
tempting berries, hidden fruit, the worry of
returning home, late.

Crossing weed encrusted lines to the
opposite platform I encounter the same old
baggage that I've come to reclaim, face
self-reproach, absolve accusations of
becoming a refugee from wells of dark intent.
I am a ghost seeking peace, I am also a
coward, leaving behind broken dreams and
idle promises as I board the next train out.

HERITAGE

The stones squat in circles, flat, distorted,
mirrors, cataracts
of a forgotten sun.

Ours is the unenviable task of assessing their
wealth, not
permitting our emotions
to show, or deny
one moment of
work probing,

if in these cold hearts beats
the vision of escape.
We need to tread carefully,
seek out signs of mortal repeated
sin, any misgiving
for days spent
in moorland
isolation.

Prometheus' children
bound in weather,
their chains of torpid heather
concealing no hero, just groping fingers of
moss to defile each crack, seek out weakness,
using rain as an alchemic lever.

Alone in the night, they show no remorse,
not one flag of surrender
as centuries of morbid bravado masks
the sighs and groans of moonlight souls
riven apart.

After all, aren't natural resources there to serve, to provide a workforce of natural heirs in a productive cycle not touched by the wishes of the majority?